SARDAR HARI SINGH NALWA

A WARRIOR WHO DEFEATED
AFGHANISTAN, THE COUNTRY WHICH WAS
NOT DEFEATED BY USA AND USSR

ISHWAR SINGH

I am dedicating this book to one of the greatest warrior in the world, Sardar Hari Singh Nalwa.

Contents

FOREWORD

Ishwar Singh have more than ten years of experience in writing story books, sakhis of devotional saints and in research activities. He is a tremendous writer. He is doing excellent job by writing about Sardar Hari Singh Nalwa. He had shown very keen interest in the field of Sikh Studies and other cultural issues.

He is also a very excellent teacher and also having deep knowledge about the social science issues. I have always seen him working very hard for his various books. He just want to express about the Indian culture to our new generations in a simple and brief manner. I wish him all the very best for his new book.

Birinder Pal Kaur

PREFACE

This book is about the brief history of Hari Singh Nalwa. The task behind to publish such content is to spread knowledge about the unsung heroes of the Sikh history among the new generation. In the schools, which are being organised by Sikh trusts, the students are just getting very limited knowledge about the Sikh warriors. Baba Banda Singh Bahadur, Baba Deep Singh etc. are the common names on the tongues of the students but they don't know about the others. This is just an effort to spread this brief information among new generations.

ACKNOWLEDGEMENTS

Writing a book is harder than I thought and more rewarding than I could have ever imagined. None of this would have been possible without my best friend, my teacher, my best motivator, my beloved mother Amarjit Kaur. She was the first who inspired me for my goals and taught me various subjects and created my interest specially in Social Sciences. She stood by me during every struggle and all my successes. Whatever I had achieved in my life it is due to my mother.

I'm eternally grateful to my father Pal Singh, who took in an extra mouth to feed when he didn't have to. He taught me discipline, tough love, manners, respect, and so much more that has helped me succeed in life. I truly have no idea where I'd be if he hadn't given me a roof over my head whom I desperately needed at that age.

To my father-in-law Narinder Singh for their moral support during the up and downs in my life. He taught me how to live positive even in the worst situations by sharing his personal experiances. He is the man who suggest me to write a book in your life because it will be your book by which you will be remembered in future.

To Dr. Davinder Singh, who never saw my age, my race, or my lack of formal education. He just saw a kid hungry to learn, hungry to grow, and hungry to succeed in teaching. He never stopped me; he only encouraged me.

Finally, to all those who have been a part of my getting there: Sukhbir Singh, Jarnail Singh, Beant Kaur, Devinder Kumar Sharma, Sumeet Kaur, Rinkpal Singh and Iqbal Singh.

Prologue

India is a country of huge cultural diversities. This diversity has its roots in the ancient and medieval period of the history. In present day life, every one is playing his role according to the role assingned by the nature. I have very much interest to explore various great warriors or personalities and cultural aspects of our Indian Society. So an idea came in my mind to explore the history of Sardar Hari Singh Nalwa. In this book, I have focused on the various achievements of Sardar Hari Singh Nalwa. I am writing this book for our younger generations so that when they will read this book, they must understand the sacrifices of our forefathers.

I
Introduction

Hari Singh Nalwa was born in the Majha area of Punjab to Dharam Kaur and Gurdial Singh Uppal in Gujranwala. Autar Singh Sandhu, a historian, asserts that Hari Singh Nalwa's family has Uppal Khatri ancestry. According to Vanit Nalwa, who claims to be Hari's descendant, their family was an Uppal Khatri and they were originally from the Amritsar-area Majitha town. His mother reared him when his father passed away in 1798. He took Amrit Sanchar in 1801, when he was ten years old, and underwent Khalsa initiation. He started overseeing his father's land when he was twelve years old and started riding horses.

His mother sent him to Ranjit Singh's court in 1804, when he was fourteen, to settle a property dispute. Due to his qualifications and history, Ranjit Singh rendered a decision in his favour in the arbitration. The Maharaja's predecessors, Maha Singh and Charat Singh, were served by Hari Singh's father and grandfather, who also shown his abilities as a horseman and musketeer. He was given a post as a personal attendant at the court by Ranjit Singh. As was traditional at the period, Hari Singh had two wives:

Raj Kaur from Rawalpindi and Desan Kaur. He has two daughters and four boys.

II
Baghmar

In 1804, a tiger attacked him while he was on a hunt, killing his horse. He reputedly killed the tiger by himself, barehanded, by tearing it apart from its mouth. His fellow hunters tried to protect him, but he rejected their offers, receiving the name Baghmar (Tiger-killer). It is uncertain if he was already serving in the military at the time of his commission as a sardar, leading 800 horses and footmen.

III

Battle of Kasur and Sialkot

In 1807, with the capture of Kasur, Hari Singh made his first substantial contribution to a Sikh conquest after taking command of an independent detachment. Due to its proximity to Ranjit Singh's capital city of Lahore, this location has long been a thorn in his side. In the fourth attempt, it was taken. Maharaja Ranjit Singh and Jodh Singh Ramgarhia were in charge of this assault. The Sardar shown incredible bravery and skill during the battle. The Sardar received a Jagir as payment for his services.

To succeed Jiwan Singh as the king of Sialkot, Ranjit Singh proposed Hari Singh Nalwa. His first conflict with a command of his own was this one. The two armies fought for a few days, but seventeen-year-old Hari Singh ultimately won. In addition to raising the Sikh flag atop the fort, Nalwa led the troops to victory.

IV
Battle of Attock

All forces crossing the Indus had a significant resupply point at the fort of Attock. This fort and the majority of the land along this frontier were controlled by Afghan appointees of the Kingdom of Kabul in the early 19th century. The Sikhs, led by Dewan Mokham Chand, the general of Maharaja Ranjit Singh, engaged Wazir Fatteh Khan and his brother Dost Mohammad Khan on behalf of Shah Mahmud of Kabul in this fight, which they ultimately prevailed in. Along with Hukam Singh Attariwala, Hari Singh Nalwa, Shyamu Singh, Khalsa Fateh Singh Ahluwalia, and Behmam Singh Malliawala, these individuals actively participated in this conflict.

The neighbouring areas of Hazara-i-Karlugh and Gandhgarh were made subservient to the Sikhs when Attock was conquered. Sherbaz Khan of Gandhgarh attempted to oppose Hari Singh Nalwa's rule in 1815 but was unsuccessful.

V
Battle of Multan

A delighted Sikh army was stationed in the Bari Doab close to Multan during the winter of 1810. They were ecstatic with their victory over the Chuj Doab. Multan's city limits were overrun without much fight, but the fort proved impossible to take. The fort was mined and bombarded without consequence. Both young Hari Singh Nalwa and Sardar Nihal Singh Attariwala suffered critical injuries. Hari Singh was burned so severely by a fire pot that was hurled from the fort's walls that it took him several months to recover enough to return to duty. The length of the siege greatly alarmed Ranjit Singh, who was forced to give up the endeavour.

Underneath the nominal leadership of Kharak Singh and the true leadership of Misr Diwan Chand, Multan was eventually conquered. Muzzaffar Khan and his sons fought valiantly to protect the area during the closely contested war, but they were unable to hold off the Sikh invasion. The capture of the fortress was "predominantly made possible" by Hari Singh Nalwa.

VI
Battle of Kashmir

The Sikh troops advanced on Kashmir in April 1819. Prince Kharak Singh was the actual commander on this occasion. In order to support the leading troops, Misr Diwan Chand commanded the forefront while Hari Singh Nalwa held up the rear. Maharaja Ranjit Singh personally oversaw the third division, which hurriedly delivered supplies to the troops in advance.

The Sikh battalions moved forward to the sound of trumpets on the morning of July 5, 1819. After a fierce battle between the two armies, the Sikhs won control of Kashmir. The Sikh camp was filled with great joy as Lahore and Amritsar were illuminated for three nights in a row. The five centuries of Muslim rule in Kashmir came to an end in this manner.

VII

Battle of Mangal and Mankera

Two years later, Hari Singh experienced his most stunning success in the Hazara region. When his tenure as governor of Kashmir came to an end successfully, he left the Valley and crossed the Kishenganga River at Muzaffarabad with 7000 foot soldiers. Hari Singh Nalwa successfully navigated the treacherous mountainous terrain, but when his group arrived in Mangal, he encountered opposition to their progress. The Jadun lord who ruled over the entire Damtaur region now made his base in Mangal, the former capital of Urasa. The tribesmen refused Hari Singh's plea for a passage through their area and wanted a charge on all the goods and treasure from Kashmir he was bringing with him. This toll was usually paid by all trade kafilas. The argument made by Hari Singh that the things he was carrying were not for commerce reasons was rejected. Parleying had failed, hence a conflict was to be fought. After collecting a fine from each home and erecting a fort nearby,

Hari Singh eventually left to join the Sikh army preparing to invade Mankera.

Mankera and Mitha Tiwana served as the primary control points for the Sindh Sagar Doab. A relative of the Durranis named Nawab Hafiz Ahmed Khan held a lot of sway in this area. He oversaw a huge territory that was guarded by 12 forts in addition to Mankera. The governors of Attock, Mankera, Mitha Tiwana, and Khushab had proclaimed their independence as Afghan administration in Kabul weakened. In 1821, Ranjit Singh celebrated Dussehra at Shahdera, across the Ravi. The area that the Maharaja had now set his sights on was most familiar to Hari Singh, the governor of Kashmir. Nalwa was urgently called to join the Lahore Army that was already travelling toward the Indus River. At Mitha Tiwana, Hari Singh Nalwa and his Kashmir squads joined the Maharaja and his troops who had already crossed the Jehlum. At the start of November, the Sikhs started their offensive operations.

With the help of 12 forts—Haidrabad, Maujgarh, Fatehpur, Pipal, Darya Khan, Khanpur, Jhandawala, Kalor, Dulewala, Bhakkar, Dingana, and Chaubara—Nawab Mohammed Khan, the predecessor of Nawab Hafiz Ahmed, had established a circle around Mankera. After the Sikh forces took control of these forts, Mankera was the only location left to be captured. The Nawab of Mankera had actively taken part in Mitha Tiwana's reduction a few years earlier. The Tiwanas, who are currently Hari Singh Nalwa's feudatories, were eager participants in repaying the Nawab for his kindness. The force was divided into three columns, one of which was commanded by Hari Singh. Each column entered Mankera territory by a unique route, taking several locations along the way before coming together close to Mankera town.

The force was divided into three columns, one of which was commanded by Hari Singh. Each caravan entered Mankera territory by a unique route, taking several locations along the way before coming together close to Mankera town. With Nalwa's men positioned to the west of the fort, Mankera was under siege.

The Nawab was given the go-ahead as jagir to travel in the direction of Dera Ismail Khan. The region was ruled by his family until 1836.

VIII
Battle of Naushehra

In 1818, the Sikhs made their first expedition into Peshawar, but they did not settle there. They were happy to only receive tribute from Yar Mohammed, the governor of the Barakzai region. Yar Mohammed's half-brother Azim Khan in Kabul resolved to lead a huge force to the border to defend Afghan honour because he utterly disagreed with the latter's respect to the Sikhs. Azim Khan wished to exact revenge on the loss of Kashmir as well as the pleas of his Peshawar comrades. In addition to 8,000 men, Khalsa Sher Singh, the Maharaja's teenage son, and Diwan Kirpa Ram were with Hari Singh Nalwa when he crossed the Indus at Attock to the Sikh post at Khairabad.

On the banks of the river Kabul, close to Nowshera, the Afghan army was anticipated (Landai). The immediate goal of Hari Singh was to take control of the Khattak region at Akora Khattak and the Yusafzai stronghold at Jehangira, which is located to the north of the Landai. The Afghan

Yusafzais put up a valiant fight against the brick fort Jehangira, which had incredibly sturdy towers. Hari Singh made his way into the fort and set up his thana there. Recrossing the Landai River, the remaining soldiers went back to their base camp at Akora. On the right bank of the Landai, facing the town of Nowshera, about ten miles to the northwest of where Hari Singh was, Mohammed Azim Khan had set up camp while waiting for Ranjit Singh to arrive. One on each bank of the Landai, the Sikhs planned two engagements.

Ranjit Singh left the fort of Attock after Hari Singh had effectively weakened the Afghan tribal strongholds on both sides of the river. He made up camp close to the Jehangira fort after fording the Landai River below Akora. The Maharaja was accompanied by the well-known military leaders Akali Phula Singh and Bal Bahadur of the Gurkhas, together with their respective armies. From the other side of the river, the Afghan Barakzais observed the conflict. The Landai river was impassable for them. The descendants of Ahmed Shah Abdali eventually left the area and headed in the direction of Jalalabad.

IX

The Last Battle of Hari Singh Nalwa

In March 1837, Nau Nihal Singh, the Maharaja's grandson, was being married. To make a strong impression on the British Commander-in-Chief, who was invited to the marriage, troops had been pulled out of the Punjab in all directions. Dost Mohammed Khan had received an invitation to the big event. Dost Mohammed had instructed his troops to march towards Jamrud along with his five sons and his chief advisors with instructions not to engage the Sikhs but rather to show strength and attempt to seize the forts of Shabqadar, Jamrud, and Peshawar. Hari Singh Nalwa was also supposed to be at Amritsar but in reality was in Peshawar.

Additionally, Hari Singh had been told to avoid conflict with the Afghans until Lahore-delivered reinforcements arrived. Mahan Singh, a lieutenant of Hari Singh, had 600 troops and scant supplies with him when he entered the Jamrud citadel. Hari Singh was in Peshawar's formidable fort. He was compelled to go to the aid of his men who were trapped in the tiny castle without water and encircled on all sides by Afghan forces. Despite the fact that the Sikhs were greatly outnumbered, Hari Singh Nalwa's presence alarmed the Afghan army. Hari Singh Nalwa was severely hurt during the fight. He instructed his lieutenant to keep his death a secret until reinforcements arrived before he passed away, and the lieutenant followed his instructions. The Afghans were aware that Hari Singh had been hurt, but they did nothing for more than a week until it was verified that he had passed away. After seeing Nalwa's body hanging outside the fort, the Afghans withdrew. In addition to defending Jamrud and Peshawar, Hari Singh Nalwa stopped the Afghans from pillaging the entire north-western boundary. As a result, he was unable to attack Afghanistan himself. This Sikh setback was expensive for the very reason that Hari Singh Nalwa's loss was irrevocable. This battle is known as Battle of Jamrud.

Ranjit Singh like to talk about the successes in fights that were won against the Afghans. By ordering a shawl from Kashmir for the then-record price of Rs 5000, on which the battles fought with them were represented, he was to immortalise these. Hari Singh Nalwa's death meant that no more conquests were accomplished in this area. Until the British occupation of the Punjab, the Khyber Pass served as the Sikh boundary.

X

A Strong Moral Character

A local Muslim woman named "Bano" had once observed the Sikhs set up camp while Hari Singh Nalwa and his troops were camped out in Jamrud, Afghanistan. She thought that Hari Singh Nalwa, the captain of the Sikhs, would be a great man to have a kid with, hopefully a boy, because she thought he was very gorgeous and attractive.

Bano visited the General one day as he was seated in his tent. Without understanding who the woman was or what she wanted, Hari Singh allowed her to enter his tent when his guards informed him that he had a native woman who wanted to see him. Bano stated: "Sikhs are a group I've heard of. You guys are amazing." I've been keeping an eye on you from a distance. Although I am single and don't have kids, I would like to have a son that is just like you."

Hari Singh reacted by saying, "May Waheguru bless you so you may have a boy with the attributes of a Sikh," not comprehending Bano's motivation or aim. "No, I want to have a son with you, Sardar Ji," Bano retorted angrily.

Replying, Hari Singh Nalwa "Dear sister! I have a husband already. I'm sorry I can't marry you or grant your wishes."

Bano cried out in disappointment as his eyes began to flood up. I had heard your Guru Nanak was magnificent and that no one leaves Guru Nanak's House empty handed, but today I am being turned away without the wish of a son being granted, she added as she turned to go.

A genuine Sikh of the Guru, Hari Singh Nalwa responded, "It is true that nobody leaves Guru Nanak's House without something. I am unable to give you a son, but if you want a son who is just like me, then accept that I will now be your son and see you as my mother."

Hari Singh Nalwa's genuineness, strong moral character, and devotion to the Guru astounded and overcame Bano. I had heard that Sikhs of the Guru are wonderful, honest people, but today I have seen it with my own eyes, the woman remarked.

Conclusion

In the political history of the Muslims, the Sikh dominance in regions long controlled by Muslims was an outlier. The worst type of humiliation that might happen to a Muslim was to be ruled by "kafirs." The Afghans had governed Kashmir for 67 years prior to the arrival of the Sikhs (1819 CE). For the Muslims, the Sikh era was the darkest in the region's history, whilst the Afghan era was the worst for the Kashmiri Pandits (Hindus). An appeal from Kashmir's Hindu people served as the impetus for the Sikh conquest of the region. Hindus who were being mistreated had had their women violated, their temples desecrated, and their cows butchered.

The Muslim clerics whipped up the populace into a frenzy by calling for "jihad" on any pretext, which made it difficult for the Sikhs who were trying to maintain calm in remote areas to open mosques and allow the call to prayer. Because it insulted the religious sensibilities of the Hindu populace, the Sikh empire executed those who killed cows. Hari Singh's strategies in Peshawar were the most effective, taking into account "the instability of the unruly tribes and the physical and political demands of the situation."